NOURISHING THE SOUL

The Real Value of Meals on Wheels

Robert U. Montgomery

RUM Publishing

Nourishing the Soul
The Real Value of Meals on Wheel
Robert U. Montgomery
RUM Publishing

Published by RUM Publishing, Bonne Terre, MO
Copyright ©2019 Robert U. Montgomery
All rights reserved.

No part of this publication may be reproduced, stored in a retrieval system, or transmitted in any form or by any means, electronic, mechanical, photocopying, recording, scanning, or otherwise, except as permitted under Section 107 or 108 of the 1976 United States Copyright Act, without the prior written permission of the Publisher. Requests to the Publisher for permission should be addressed to Permissions Department, RUM Publishing, roticomontgomery@gmail.com.

Limit of Liability/Disclaimer of Warranty: While the publisher and author have used their best efforts in preparing this book, they make no representations or warranties with respect to the accuracy or completeness of the contents of this book and specifically disclaim any implied warranties of merchantability or fitness for a particular purpose. No warranty may be created or extended by sales representatives or written sales materials. The advice and strategies contained herein may not be suitable for your situation. You should consult with a professional where appropriate. Neither the publisher nor author shall be liable for any loss of profit or any other commercial damages, including but not limited to special, incidental, consequential, or other damages.

Cover and Interior design: Davis Creative, www.DavisCreative.com

Library of Congress Cataloging-in-Publication Data

Library of Congress Control Number: 2019905878

Robert U. Montgomery

Nourishing the Soul: The Real Value of Meals on Wheel

ISBN: 978-1-7330033-1-5

Library of Congress subject headings:

1. BIO000000 Biography & Autobiography / General   2. OCC019000 Body, Mind & Spirit / Inspiration & Personal Growth   3. HEA048000 Health & Fitness / Diet & Nutrition / General

2019

This book is dedicated to Dorothy Lorraine Gouin and all of the other volunteers who sustain the Meals on Wheels program.

Bonne Terre Director Cher Robinson and Park Hills Director Holly Buxton deserve special recognition too for going above and beyond nearly every day at their senior centers, as do the cooks for the long hours they spend preparing good food, five days a week. (I especially like the Mexican!)

For author Robert U. Montgomery, this book is a labor of love. All proceeds from Nourishing the Soul will be donated to Meals on Wheels programs.

A special thanks to St. Louis-based Davis Creative for its generous assistance in the design of this book.

Table of Contents

Part I: Dorothy Lorraine Gouin 1
  Chapter 1: A Life in Service 3
  Chapter 2: 'She Is the Sweetest!'. 11
  Chapter 3: Recognition 15
  Chapter 4: Hometown Girl 19

Part II: For What It's Worth **29**
  Chapter 5: Nourishing Souls as Well as Bodies. . . . 31
  Chapter 6: 'The Meals Mean More Than
    You Can Ever Know' 39
  Chapter 7: Barely Hanging On at Home. 49
  Chapter 8: The Normal Delivery That
    Became Much More. 55
  Chapter 9: 'An Orange Can Elicit
    the Biggest Smile' 57
  Chapter 10: Science Says Volunteering
    Really Is Good for You 63
  Chapter 11: Empathy and Smiles. 67
  Chapter 12: Four-Legged Friends. 71
  Chapter 13: Why We Volunteer 79

Part III: Center Stage **91**
  Chapter 14: What You're Missing 93
  Chapter 15: Senior Center Facts 101
  Chapter 16: The Quiet Man. 107
  Chapter 17: Aging Matters 113
  Chapter 18: Who Is Eligible for Meals? 115
  Chapter 19: Bonne Terre Center History. 117
  About the Author 119

Part I
Dorothy Lorraine Gouin

Chapter 1

A Life in Service

Volunteer Dorothy Gouin at her home away from home for more than 19 years.

Our hair thins and our middles thicken. Wrinkles arise. We limp. We groan. And suddenly one day, we look in the mirror and are stunned to see that we are old!

Well, old on the outside anyway. On the inside, we still feel the same as we always did. It is the outside that has betrayed us.

Some go quietly. They tell themselves, "I'm old. I guess that I should act like it." They settle into easy chairs and await the inevitable.

Dorothy Lorraine Gouin isn't one of them.

At 95, she's still volunteering four or five days at week at the Senior and Nutrition Center in Bonne Terre, Mo. And she started a few years after she returned to her hometown at 73, an age when so many have been nestled for years in their easy chairs. She also helps out at a local food pantry and does other charitable work.

Dorothy is a voracious reader and delights in doing number puzzles to keep her mind sharp. She still drives, and only recently had her license renewed. Her only concession to age is a cane that she mostly needs to get up and down steps.

"So many people's lives have been touched by her," said Jeainia Jennings, who delivers Meals on Wheels with her husband, Mike, and has become a close friend to Dorothy in recent years. "People we deliver to ask us all the time how Dorothy is doing."

Center Director Cher Robinson added, "Her loving smile immediately grabs you. She gives hugs with the most deliberate intention of making you feel better. You wouldn't realize you really needed her hug until she let go."

With a laugh Jeainia added, "I get such a kick out of her! You can't help but marvel at all she does and what a feisty little lady she is."

She is indeed. I don't remember the first person I met at the center when I volunteered to deliver meals back in 2011. But Dorothy is the first person that I remember. She seemed to be a white-haired, Smurf-size version of my Army drill sergeant.

She was a youthful 87 back then, when she took me on a delivery run to show me how it's done, including filling out the minimal, but important paperwork. She sometimes delivered meals on several different routes during the week, taking over wherever she was needed, and that included to remote, rural locations, even during wintry weather.

Today, she occasionally helps out at the reception desk, but mostly she supervises the schedule sheets for six routes, confirming that meals are delivered or, if not, why not. And, if you're delivering meals, you had better be certain the numbers align and you've signed each sheet.

Otherwise Dorothy will show you the error of your ways and make certain that you know how to do things correctly the next time.

As do I, Mike Jennings knows what it means to be schooled by Dorothy. He laughed and said, "One of her favorite words is 'so.'"

As in, "So… this is what you should do." Another is "basically," as in "Basically, this is where you screwed up."

As the oldest of eight children, Dorothy readily admits that she was and remains "bossy," but it is a bossy that endears her to everyone because she cares so much about doing her job properly—and making certain that we do so as well.

"For how old she is, Dorothy is amazing. She always knows us by name. She's always pleasant," said Rena Ziegler, who, with husband, Al, has been delivering meals for 16 years.

"She's part of our family here at the center," Cher said. "The first time she didn't show up

Part I: Dorothy Lorraine Gouin

at her routine time, we immediately started a search party.

"She's so independent. She didn't imagine that others would worry about her. From that day forward, she notifies us if she has an appointment or another engagement that would delay her arriving at her usual time," the director added.

When she's not attending to center business, Dorothy works on those puzzles or balancing her checking account.

"She has the most peculiar checking account system I've ever seen," said Clara, the youngest of her siblings.

"She's there for hours working on that damn checkbook," Jeainia laughed.

But when you listen to Dorothy explain how she figures out patterns in the puzzles, it's easy to understand that her grasp of mathematics exceeds those of us many years younger.

"I love numbers," Dorothy said. "I've been dealing with them all my life. I worked in an office doing accounting when I was in the WAC (Women's Army Corps) and that's what

I'm doing at the center. That's why I like the puzzles too."

But at age 95, why not just settle into that easy chair at home to do the puzzles and balance the checkbook?

"I like volunteering. I like helping others. And I love coming here," she explained. "And what I do here (at the center), I've been doing all my life, and I want to keep doing it."

"So"—as Dorothy would say—the center is her home away from home.

And when she's there, according to Jeainia, "She always wants to introduce you to people. She wants to make sure everyone knows everyone else."

At 20 years or more older than many of us, Dorothy is our favorite teacher, our foster mother, the person whom we most look forward to seeing whenever we go into the center.

When she's not there, she probably is helping out at the food pantry or doing other charitable work. "She delivers church newsletters (to St. Joe Manor care facility) and visits

Alzheimer's patients she doesn't even know," Jeainia said.

Reflecting the importance of religion to her, Dorothy has a cross on her desk at the center. "She frequently sits with her elbows on her desk, hands up and fingers intertwined under her chin, her head bowed down, and whispers her requests," Cher said. "Each time someone associated with the center becomes ill, she is sure to ask for healing."

Dorothy also attends mass often. Mike and Jeainia suspect that she sits in the same pew that her family occupied nearly a century ago. She leaves her prayer book and other items under the cushion and has given strict instructions to the couple not to move them when they clean the church.

"She's so religious and such a good person," Jeainia said. "When she dies, snap! She will be up there with God."

But sister Clara said that Dorothy intends to be around awhile longer. "She plans to live to be one hundred," she explained.

And she intends to remain as independent as she can enroute to that goal.

"At 95, it's pretty cool all that she can do," Jeainia said. "But she realizes that she can't do everything. A lot of the time when we're walking, I'll put my arm around her. She's so precious."

Dorothy grudgingly admits that sometimes she does need assistance, but other times, she's just being polite.

"A lot of people today ask if they can help me," she chuckled. "And I'll tell them, 'If you want.'"

Cher concluded, "Some might say she's a legacy. She's been here approximately 19 years, helping, guiding, teaching, listening, and most of all loving all who have met her. I believe Dorothy is an angel."

Chapter 2

'She Is the Sweetest!'

Mike and Jeainia Jennings with Dorothy at Bonne Terre center's annual Christmas Party.

People in her hometown of Bonne Terre immediately showed their love for Dorothy when I posted photos of her on Facebook and mentioned that I was featuring her in a book

Nourishing the Soul

about Meals on Wheels. Here are some of their comments:

- "You were a beautiful young lady and are still a beautiful person."
  –Sis Smith
- "Angel."
  –Stanley Perry
- "I love Dorothy! See her at mass sometimes. She was a friend of my Mom."
  –Meri Wann Stephens.
- "Good woman."
  –Charles Pace.
- "She is the sweetest!"
  –Shannon Casteel-Williams
- "She and my mother went to grade school together and Dorothy visited her at St. Joe Manor (assisted-living facility) all the time. What an amazing woman!"
  –Barbara Compton Dobbins.
- "Wow, she is a good woman."
  –Roger and Carolyn Hogan.

Part I: Dorothy Lorraine Gouin

- "Great, admirable woman."
  –G. Henry Moon.
- "They just don't make them like that anymore. What a jewel!"
  –Madeline Carver.

Chapter 3

Recognition

Director Cher Robinson watches as Dorothy draws name of quilt winner at Bonne Terre center's annual quilt show and bake sale.

My good friend Dorothy has been recognized in the media at least twice for her nearly two decades of volunteer service.

In 2012, she was one of 34 who received Missouri's Lieutenant Governor's Senior Service Awards at the Capitol in Jefferson City, Mo. More recently, the *Daily Journal* newspaper wrote about her when St. Vincent de

Paul Food Pantry celebrated her 95 birthday on March 26, 2019.

The newspaper described her as a "long-time and revered volunteer," reporting that, every Friday, Gouin fills bags "with goods like ground beef, pork, steak, and other frozen products."

It added, "Gouin volunteers in other places, and is busy almost every day of the week."

A pantry spokesperson said, "We've got a lot of wonderful volunteers, but she's been here for about 20 years."

And volunteer Al Luebbers added, "Some us see her as a legend in this town."

Dorothy told the newspaper that volunteering "keeps me from being alone.

"I enjoy doing it," she continued. "I also volunteer at St. Joe Manor and the (Bonne Terre Senior and) Nutrition Center. I do office work at the center and help deliver the (church) newsletter to residents at St. Joe Manor."

In Jefferson City seven years before, Lt. Gov. Peter Kinder said that Dorothy "sets an example for all Missourians with her kindness and willingness to serve her community tirelessly.

"Her selfless service is an inspiration to all who know her."

As a youthful woman of 88, Dorothy managed the center's route sheets, kept track of those who ate at the center, and often delivered meals on two routes, according to then Director Karah Cain.

"Dorothy is here with me every single day," she said. "She's always willing to take on other routes if it fits in with the other stuff she does.

"She's quite a woman. She's my only female veteran. She has an ongoing need to serve and stay busy."

Cain added that Dorothy is crucial to the operation of the center, pointing out that "she has been sick only one time since I've been here and, boy, did we miss her."

In nominating the World War II veteran for the award, Cain pointed out that "Dorothy is a small but mighty woman who comes from an era of hard-working individuals. Without Dorothy, our center wouldn't as good as it is."

In addition to her work at the center in 2012, Dorothy also accompanied the priest from St. Joseph Catholic Church to celebrate mass at a local prison, as well as helped out at the food pantry and visited residents at St. Joe Manor assisted-living facility.

Chapter 4

Hometown Girl

Dorothy's family, longtime residents of Bonne Terre, during World War II. She is top row, center, in her U.S. Army uniform.

Theodore and Ernestine Gouin arrived in Bonne Terre in 1924, just 15 days after the birth of their first of eight children, Dorothy Lorraine, in Philadelphia, Pa. Theodore then worked as a metallurgist for St. Joe Lead Company until his retirement in 1962.

Dorothy's father was a self-taught chemist from Quebec, Canada, and her mother, who was of Acadian descent, was from New Hampshire, she told Mike and Jeainia Jennings and me one day during lunch at the Bonne Terre Senior and Nutrition Center.

"My father went to New Orleans to apply for a job," she said. "And I guess that they sent him here."

The four of us often have lunch together, after Mike, Jeainia and I deliver meals. Usually, though, other people join us, and two or three conversations are going on at the same time. And with Dorothy's hearing not as good at it once was, conversing with her was difficult.

On this day, though, we were lucky. The four of us had a table to ourselves.

"I was a tomboy," our 95-year-old friend said. "When boys would come to play with my brothers, I'd take their bikes and ride them around town. And I played baseball."

As the oldest, she played teacher as well with four sisters and three brothers. "I'd ask them questions, and, if they answered correctly, they got to move up the steps," she explained.

Part I: Dorothy Lorraine Gouin

When she admitted that she had been bossy, I revealed that she reminded me of my drill sergeant in the Army when we first met. Dorothy laughed and said, "And I'm still bossy."

With great good humor, her sister Clara echoed that sentiment when we got together to talk about her oldest sibling.

"During my confirmation (in 1950), we were at the rail in church. Dorothy was my sponsor so she was behind me.

"And she whacked me so hard on my shoulder that I never forgot it!" she said.

"That's why she did it," Clara added with a smile. "So I'd never forget (to be respectful)."

Clara was only 6 years old when Dorothy joined the Women's Army Corps (WAC) in 1944 and recalled that her "take charge" attitude hadn't changed when she came home to visit.

"Boy, was she mean!"

But she added that there was a softer and artistic side to her sister as well. "She loved to dance and took lessons from Arthur Murray. And she tried to play the accordion," Clara said, hinting that the latter didn't turn our quite so well as the former.

•••

Brother and Sister Are Serving Uncle Sam

During April 1944, a local newspaper reported the following:

"Pvt. Lorraine Gouin, 20, joined the WACs February 20th and reported for active duty at the Army Post Branch, Des Moines, Iowa, April 4th. Prior to entering service, she was employed at Rice Stix Shirt Factory in this city. Pvt. Gouin attended the local schools and was a member of the graduating class of the BTHS in 1942."

It added that Dorothy's brother, Theodore, 18, was in his senior year of high school when he enlisted in the U.S. Navy on Nov. 3, 1943 and was sent to Sheepshead Bay in New York.

The newspaper later reported that a second brother, Robert, enlisted in the U.S. Army to served in the Armored Cavalry and was posted to Fort Riley in Kansas for training.

Part I: Dorothy Lorraine Gouin

A glamorous Dorothy during her younger years.

After four years of service in the military, where her sisters-in-arms nicknamed her "Pee Wee," Dorothy moved to Massachusetts, living there until she returned to Bonne Terre in 1997 and bought the family home.

That day at lunch, Dorothy surprisingly talked a little about those nearly 50 years that she lived out of state. During past lunches, she never had, possibly because her long-time "significant other," Ernie, died there shortly before she came back home.

In fact, just the mention of his name brought tears to her eyes, as she talked about him and their life together. She showed us photos of the two of them as a couple.

They lived in Springfield, Mass., sister Clara said, where Dorothy worked as a bookkeeper for Abdow's, which once owned the Big Boy chain of restaurants. She added that she and sister Barbara followed Dorothy to Massachusetts and lived there for awhile as well.

"Dorothy loved to cook," she remembered. "And she was a good cook."

After she returned to Bonne Terre, Clara said, Dorothy continued to cook, although she lived alone. She prepared meals for those in need whom she had befriended, as well as drove them places, such as to church and the grocery store.

As she talked to Mike, Jeainia, and me at lunch, Dorothy seemed most to enjoy reminiscing about her childhood in Bonne Terre. She told us about Alma Bailey's Lingerie Shop and nearby Bailey's Arts & Crafts, owned by her husband, Linus. She recalled a swimming pool behind the post office and Odean Theater, where she and other youngsters watched Flash Gordon on Saturdays.

As we finished lunch, Dorothy said, "I usually just sit and listen. Today, I'm doing all the talking.

"It's fun. It helps me remember a lot of things that I'd forgotten about."

In Dorothy's Own Words

In 2014, the town of Bonne Terre celebrated its sesquicentennial with publication of a book, *Bonne Terre, Missouri*, about its history and its most prominent families, including Dorothy's.

Here's are some excerpts from her contribution:

"I went to St. Joseph Catholic School, which had four classrooms, two grades to each room.

"When I was in first grade, the nuns told Mom and Dad to speak English to be, because they did not want me speaking French. The Ursuline nuns taught the Three R's, reading, 'riting, and 'rithmetic, and good penmanship.

"We had spelling bees between the different grades and we stood in front of class for recitations—a great experience for later years…

"Mom always had a garden and raised chickens. She would take her vegetables and sometimes eggs into town and barter for other things that we needed, such as meat, cheese, etc.

"I graduated from elementary school in 1938 and from high school in 1942. We had our prom at what is now Heritage Hall.

"I worked at the Rice Stix Shirt Factory for a year and Mary Jean, my sister, at the telephone company, both located behind the Commerce Bank…

"My sister Helen worked at Karthan's Hotel and Cafe, where they had buses running daily. I remember once when I walked from Bonne Terre to Flat River, waiting for the bus to catch up with me. It never did…"

And about her time in Massachusetts, she said the following:

"Discharged after four years (in the military), I had the opportunity to go east to

Part I: Dorothy Lorraine Gouin

Springfield, Mass. I spoke to Mom and she said I might as well go there; there were no jobs at home.

"I stayed with a family for seven years, taking care of the semi-invalid mother, while the sisters went to work. I later got another job and found an apartment.

"Mom sent the two younger girls, Barbara and Clara to live with me, which they did until they married."

Part II
For What It's Worth

Chapter 5

Nourishing Souls as Well as Bodies

Volunteers bring more than meals to those on their routes.

I started delivering Meals on Wheels in early 2011. I didn't give any thought to why except that it seemed a good thing to do and I suspected that I might be getting a little too old to be a Big Brother for a second time.

And, I'm embarrassed to say, I have no idea when the light bulb finally went on above my head and I realized that the program is far more significant and meaningful than its name suggests— both for those who distribute the meals and those who receive them.

But it is. Of that I have no doubt. I know that because I am a better person than I was in early 2011. Oh, I still am a very flawed individual. But I am kinder, more forgiving, more patient, more generous, and more thoughtful because of my participation in the program. Other volunteers are as well, I'm confident.

Of course, it's entirely possible than some were that way before they started participating and I met them. Perhaps some of their goodness rubbed off on me. In fact, I think that it's likely. On the other hand, I hope that I haven't corrupted them too much in return! I'm afraid that I might have.

Still, I also know that what I have seen and experienced as I've delivered thousands of meals have made me more grateful for what I have and more giving as a consequence.

Part II: For What It's Worth

Here's a small example:

Recently I was behind a man at the checkout line in the grocery store. He was buying meat, bread, and other basics. But when the cashier told him the cost, he told her to take back some items.

Now, I like to think that I would have stepped in to help before I started delivering Meals on Wheels. But what I know for certain is that participation in the program has made me far more appreciative of my blessings and willing to share them with others. I didn't pause to consider whether I should "get involved," as I might have previously. The old me would have engaged in an internal debate, one side saying that the man just didn't want to spend that much money and the other arguing that maybe he wanted the items but didn't have enough to pay for them.

And by the time the debate was finished, the man would have returned some items, paid for the rest, and left the store.

Instead, I just acted. I told the cashier that I would pay the difference.

As the man exited, thanking me for the third time, the clerk handed me my receipt, showing me that he hadn't been able to pay because he didn't have enough credit remaining on his food stamps card.

Here's another:

As I drove along a street busy with traffic, I spied a woman that I recognized from the senior apartments where I deliver meals. Although probably old enough to qualify and hearing impaired, she wasn't a participant in the program. But we had said hello to each other from time to time.

A slightly built woman, she had purchased a table at a thrift store, which was across that busy street from the apartments, and was slowly pushing it downhill in the massive parking lot toward that traffic. Her intent was sadly clear and frightening. With no other alternative, she was going to try to manhandle the table across the road, despite nearly nonstop traffic from both directions.

I took a quick right into the parking lot, made certain that she knew who I was, and

Part II: For What It's Worth

communicated as best I could that I would help. I loaded the table in my car, opened the passenger door for her, and drove her home, where I unloaded the table and took it inside.

Over the years, I've also fixed vacuum cleaners—or attempted to anyway—and opened pill bottles. I've moved furniture, adjusted television settings, bought cantaloupes for a sweet, little man who couldn't afford them, and given rides to those who didn't or couldn't drive and needed to get to appointments or buy necessities.

Also, I've realized that some people need the human contact as much as they need the food, and I might be the only one that they talk to that day.

John (not his real name) seemed to be one of them. When I knocked on his door, he asked me to bring the meal inside, as he remained in his recliner. Dizzy spells, he explained early on, made it nearly impossible for him to be on his feet for any length of time, with some days much worse than others.

After I sat the meal down, he always said, "What's going on in town?"

The first time he asked, he caught me off guard and unable to answer because I live about eight miles outside of town and really didn't pay much attention. But prompted by his interest, I started being more observant and asking around so I could tell him, detailing such "news," as street repairs, storm damage, and construction of a new building for the fire department. In turn, he told me how things used to be by comparison. While he was happy to hear the latest news and gossip, I twice benefitted, becoming more informed about my own community so I could tell John and becoming more educated about its history from him.

Then one day, for a reason that I can't remember, he told me the reason that he so looked forward to me telling him what was going on is that he hadn't been outside his house in more than two years because of the dizzy spells.

I managed my usual cheerful "See you next week," but inside I was grief-stricken to learn that this otherwise healthy looking man was a prisoner in his own home. I cried when I got back inside my car.

Pets and sports are the most frequent topics of conversation, as well as the weather, of course. Many of those who receive meals have canine companions and, because I bring treats, many of those dogs have become my best buddies. Their eager antics when they see me, knowing what I have in my pocket, make all of us smile.

Sports talk usually includes an analysis of the previous game for the St. Louis Cardinals or Blues and what their chances are in the next one. One of my Meals on Wheels friends showed me his autographs of baseball legends Yogi Berra and Joe Garagiola and shared with me the stories of how he acquired them. I suspect that he enjoyed reliving those pleasurable moments as much as I did hearing about them.

Although I'm no expert on the subject, I suspect that having someone to talk to feeds their souls just as Meals on Wheels feeds their bodies.

I know that I'm not alone among the volunteers in helping out and staying for a few minutes to chat. Doing more than just handing them their meals nourishes our souls as well as theirs.

My point is that many of the people I've met on my routes become more than just meal recipients. They become friends. We discover and talk about common interests. Because of their age and/or disabilities, I see some struggle with things that I can help them with, and I am happy to do so. Everything that I do for them reminds me of how fortunate I am, which is why I am a better person—and not just when I'm delivering meals, but in all aspects of my life.

Chapter 6

'The Meals Mean More Than You Can Ever Know'

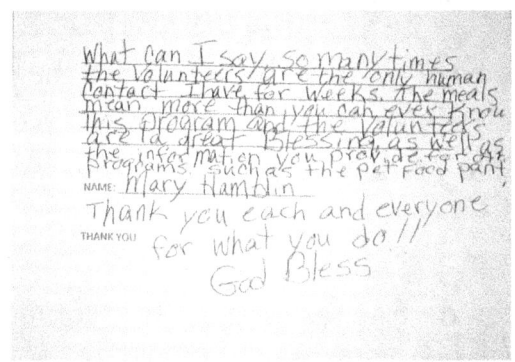

Volunteers are not paid—not because they are worthless, but because they are priceless.

Cher Robinson, director of the Bonne Terre Senior and Nutrition Center, asked meal recipients for feedback about the Meals on Wheels program. The following are some of their written comments:

•••

"After finding out I have terminal cancer, the meals really help me. Most days, I don't have the energy to cook. Although some friends mean well, everyone can't cook. I do appreciate everything that people do. God bless you all."

•••

"We have enjoyed the meals and the volunteers have been friendly and polite. We especially like Miss Nancy S. She is the sweetest lady."

•••

"They do fine (as long as they come to the second door)."

•••

"I really appreciate the meals I have been receiving. They are always good and the volunteers are always nice. Without them, I couldn't receive the meals."

•••

"Your volunteers do an awesome job. They are friendly and caring. We thank you all so very much. And God bless."

•••

Part II: For What It's Worth

"Thank you all for each delivery that you have made. I have enjoyed it. And I hope the bags that I give you guys help you."

•••

"I can't put in words how nice and helpful all the workers who bring the lunches are. I appreciate also all who manage to cook and perform the many jobs that must be done to make this a success."

•••

"What can I say? So many times the volunteers are the only human contact I have for weeks. The meals mean more than you can ever know. This program and the volunteers are a great blessing and so is the information that you provide for other programs, such as the pet food pantry. Thank you to each and every one for what you do."

•••

"I love getting my meals and the folks are so nice. They do need to knock louder or ring the bell. Other than that, no problem. I love it."

•••

"We love the meals and the volunteers are nice and polite. They are always on time with the meals. We really do appreciate them."

•••

> After finding out I am terminal with cancer, the meals really help me, most days I don't have the energy to cook. Although some meals I can't mean well everyone can't cook. I do appreciate anything that people do.
>
> NAME: Alice Wilbanks
> THANK YOU
> God Bless you all

"The volunteers are very helpful since I don't drive or have a car. The volunteers are very friendly, always smiling, even in the worst weather. I so appreciate what they do every day throughout the year."

•••

"I really appreciate your food service and the kindly volunteers who take time out of their day to help deliver the food. We really thank you."

•••

"On a fixed income, every little bit helps. So the love they have shown is above measure. May God bless every one of them."

•••

"The meal program helps to ensure that I get a hot meal each day. Without it, I'd be eating a lot of sandwiches. Thank you to all of the volunteers that make this possible. I can't tell you enough how much I appreciate you all!"

•••

"We love the meals and the volunteers are nice and polite. They are always on time with the meals. We really do appreciate the workers."

•••

"The people who deliver my meals are so wonderful and friendly and have the biggest smiles. I want to thank every one of them and all of you who make the meals."

•••

"The seniors who deliver our meals are very kind and helpful. All our volunteers have been outstanding. No matter what the weather is outside, they always have a warm smile. P.S. I like to thank the ladies who make our lunches and for your program. It's very helpful to all of us."

•••

"All of my volunteers are friendly and kind and always have a smile on their face even when the weather is really bad. And Shirley who comes every Friday is so sweet. I really love to see her. My husband cannot write, so this letter is for both of us."

•••

"God bless all of you for volunteering to bring lunch. I have terminal cancer. I have limited funds and sometimes can't even afford toilet paper toiletries, etc. I have my service dog, Bootsy. I try to save money for her shots. I do without things I need to give her proper food and vet care.

"You bringing me warm, healthy meals, I am so grateful to you for finding the time to help the older, less fortunate folks such as I. It's scary being older and not knowing how much longer I have to be around to watch my grandbabies grow up."

Part II: For What It's Worth

•••

"We love Meals on Wheels! The people who deliver our meals are very friendly and they have a positive attitude. Thank you, Meals on Wheels."

•••

"Every day I can count on a nutritious meal. The thing that is as important are the people that deliver the meals. They always arrive with a smile and kind words, regardless of the weather. Thank you all so much. God bless you."

•••

"Meals on Wheels helps me keep from going hungry. Thanks a lot."

•••

"I appreciate all the volunteers. Nancy, Al, and Rena have been a blessing. They always come to my home and make me smile. I am so very grateful to have meals delivered."

•••

"The meals are great and help improve my health. They deliver on time every day. They're friendly!"

Just the Facts

The importance of the Meals on Wheels program to millions is confirmed by the following from Meals on Wheels America:

- 59 percent of home-delivered meal recipients live alone, and for many of them, the person delivering the meal is often the only person they will see that day.
- 9 out of 10 recipients say Meals on Wheels helps them feel more secure.
- 9 out of 10 say Meals on Wheels helps them live independently.
- Meals on Wheels can serve a senior for an entire year for the same cost as just one day in a hospital or 10 days in a nursing home.

Here's Who Benefits:

- 59 percent of home-delivered meal recipients are 75 or older.
- 69 percent are women.
- 15 percent are veterans.
- 59 percent live alone.
- 25 percent live in rural areas.
- 35 percent live at poverty level.
- 28 percent are a racial and/or ethnic minority.
- 46 percent self-report fair or poor health.
- 82 percent take 3 or more medications daily.

Chapter 7
Barely Hanging On at Home

Meals on Wheels program helps many live longer and happier lives in their own homes.

Nourishing the Soul

By Sammie Justesen

(Editor's note: Sammie is a good friend and fellow writer. She and her husband, Dee, have devoted much of their lives to helping others, as well as abandoned and abused animals.)

In a small, tidy house in the mountains of eastern Kentucky, I learned to love a couple in their 90's who still lived at home—barely. Harold was blind and feeble, but able to get around with a cane. His wife, Ethel, could no longer walk or care for herself and spent her time in a hospital bed situated in the living room so she could see most of the house. She used her vision to guide Harold while he felt his way around and took care of things. Their grown kids came on weekends to do major chores, but they spent much time on their own.

Ethel was tiny, fragile, and as sweet as the honeysuckle that bloomed outside the front door. She never complained and had kind words for everyone. Harold was tall and lanky with a shock of white hair that stood on end,

Part II: For What It's Worth

since he couldn't see to comb it. He shared Ethel's happy disposition.

As their home-care nurse, I came every week to assess living conditions and keep them on track with medication, doctor's appointments, and Ethel's frequent skin breakdown. There was talk of a nursing home, but Harold and Ethel begged everyone to let them stay in the home they loved. As case manager, I supervised a team of people who made this possible: Home-care aides came daily to bathe Ethel and help with housework. A physical therapist helped with safety and mobility. The hospital we worked for delivered oxygen and other supplies as needed. Respiratory therapists monitored the oxygen and checked Ethel's breathing status.

But what about food and nutrition, that most basic human need? Harold and Ethel were at risk for tumbling down a slippery slope that begins with food. Many senior citizens exist on snack foods, can't shop for healthy food, forget to eat, and/or skip meals. Malnutrition exacerbates health issues until they end up in assisted-care facilities for want of regular, nutritious food.

Harold could prepare rudimentary meals, but nothing fancy, and good nutrition was key to keeping them at home. Meals on Wheels to the rescue! Five days a week a volunteer arrived with hot, delicious food prepared in a kitchen miles away. Kentucky cooks are wonderful and I envied the meals they received— not frozen dinners, but lovingly prepared home cooking.

Meals on Wheels helped my patients on many levels. Harold and Ethel adored the kind volunteers who quickly became their friends. These friendships, the lingering smell of delicious food, and knowing people cared about them warmed the hearts— and stomachs— of this lonely couple.

"The best part of our day is when they bring the food," Ethel told me. "We look forward to it all morning, wondering what we'll get to eat. And they always bring enough for supper. Our volunteer, John, tells us about his kids and we feel like he's part of the family."

"What's your favorite?" I asked.

Part II: For What It's Worth

"Beans and cornbread," Harold said. "I grew up on beans and cornbread."

"Peach cobbler!" Ethel answered. "They make it just like I used to."

That's another thing—for most of us—food is tied to warm memories of childhood and family. Thanks to the volunteers at Meals on Wheels for making life better for so many people!

Chapter 8

The Normal Delivery That Became Much More

By Barb and Del Weinhold
(Editor's note: Barb and Del Weinhold deliver Meals on Wheels for the Bonne Terre Senior and Nutrition Center)

It started out as a normal Meals on Wheels delivery. After we rang the doorbell to the modest home, Jerri (not her real name) answered with a smile. Not a part of our usual route, she was a white-haired lady dragging an oxygen tank behind her.

After she genuinely thanked us for the meal, we introduced ourselves and then went on our way, thinking no more about it.

Several months later, we again were assigned to do the route that she was on. This time, she told us that she no longer had custody of her grandchildren, because of her failing health. She mentioned that her daughter Olivia was in the Women's Correctional Facility at Vandalia, Mo. We shared that we had a friend there also.

Several months later, we received a message from our friend at Vandalia, saying that she was sharing a room with none other than Olivia, Jerri's daughter! At a facility with thousands of residents, that was an amazing coincidence. Or was it?

Our friend asked if we could we deliver a yellow rose to Olivia's mother who was in the Intensive Care Unit at our local hospital. Of course, we told her that we would.

As we entered the hospital room, another daughter graciously accepted the yellow rose, saying that her mom, who appeared to be sleeping, just loved them!

At her request, we then sent a photo of Jerri and the rose to Olivia so that she would know that her gesture of love had been received.

What started as a normal Meals on Wheels delivery on a route that we normally didn't cover turned into something far more significant and meaningful than we ever could have imagined.

Chapter 9

'An Orange Can Elicit the Biggest Smile'

Often a Meals on Wheels volunteer is the only person a recipient will see during the day.

Nourishing the Soul

By Steve Kohler
(Editor's note: Steve and Peggy Kohler deliver Meals on Wheels for the Bonne Terre Senior and Nutrition Center.)

It's tiny, really. Less than two percent of our waking week and a couple of bucks in gas to drive 22 miles delivering 20 meals. So our contribution to Meals on Wheels doesn't budge the needle of what we could (and should) be doing as contributing citizens.

But for participants, one good meal a day might be critically important. The cost and effort of getting a good meal when you're aging, living alone or infirm, could be overwhelming, if what we see is representative. Sometimes, in 21st century America, where everyone should be able to make ends meet, the ends can be a long way apart. It's disturbing and it's wrong.

The meals are always fresh and well balanced — proteins, carbohydrates, fruits. Expert cooks and meal planners see to that. Contact with someone at the door who displays concern, asks about your health, and wishes you a good

Part II: For What It's Worth

day could be uplifting. I'm not claiming that it is, mind you, or that we always say the right thing, but just maybe it's a bright spot.

So we do it to provide a little help and comfort to people who need it. We do it because we feel grateful and a little guilty to have so much. Unacknowledged privilege leads straight to a sense of entitlement, and entitlement is a disgusting human foible.

We also do it for the education. Much of America appears before us. A broad spectrum of human nature is represented in two hours. Some people say nothing, just take the package that we extend and retreat. Even after years of answering the door for us, they have no response when we wish them a good weekend. Others are deeply grateful for the simple meal. An orange can elicit the biggest smile.

A few people may be gaming the system, with a Lincoln in the drive and central air and fine furniture. But we've learned not to judge, because we're not aware of the underlying circumstances. Who knows, they may be making a huge contribution to the program.

Besides, hardship and need come in every guise. Each person's is different. Our task is simple, and we try to keep it that way.

But sometimes, the responsibility broadens. We visit one house—a well-kept mobile home—where the woman lives alone and travels in an electric chair. Her place is not on Easy Street, but her spirit is always bright and pleasant, and she always has news of family or shared acquaintances for us.

Her mailbox is full of notes destined for family members put there when she collected the incoming mail. On one occasion, she asked if the Nutrition Center that operates Meals on Wheels could use a donation, and we ended up taking a 50-pound dehumidifier from her, along with baskets full of clothes and other contributions. She never fails to say a big "Thank you" and to bless us.

Two months ago, a stray, collarless dog showed up at her place and settled in. She and her sister looked for an owner as best they could but found none. They started feeding the dog, which put on weight and began to wag her tail.

Part II: For What It's Worth

The prognosis was that she would soon have pups. Clearly, our friend couldn't care for new puppies. As whelping time neared, we found a vet facility that could help, rounded up the dog, then made a small donation for the dog's care. That stray dog is missed by all of us, but we agreed that there was only one solution. The staff at the veterinary facility named her after our Meals on Wheels friend.

We first signed up to deliver meals when we saw a public plea for volunteers that said the program would have to close if more people didn't step up to help. That seemed simply wrong. So were our expectations. Now, every week, we visit some of our townspeople, get an education, collect many warm wishes, share an occasional laugh, and derive a small but good feeling.

Chapter 10
Science Says Volunteering Really Is Good for You

Meals on Wheels volunteers are a happy bunch!

Yeah, most all of us know that helping others makes us feel good. But studies are showing something even more significant: Volunteering produces tangible mental and physical benefits, including lowering blood pressure and reducing feelings of depression. Speaking as someone who lives alone and doesn't have the active social life that I once had, I can say emphatically that the latter definitely is true for me.

"Research has shown that there's evidence volunteer work promotes psychological well being," said Rodlescia Sneed, a public health research associate at Michigan State University who has studied the impacts of volunteering. "In my own work, I've shown it's linked to improvements in factors like depressive symptoms, purpose in life, and feelings of optimism."

Although this field of investigation is relatively new, research has revealed that oxytocin, a neurotransmitter that regulates social interaction, spikes in some people who regularly volunteer, helping them manage stressful events.

Sneed added that researchers more and more believe that volunteering is beneficial because it allows you to focus on something else for while. It also puts your life in perspective compared to those being helped. In other words, your own life doesn't seem so bad when you're delivering meals to homebound seniors who might not otherwise have enough to eat.

Part II: For What It's Worth

Sadly, I suspect, some don't volunteer because they fear that doing so will make their lives more stressful, adding responsibility and reducing time for relaxation. In reality, it's the opposite. I've yet to meet someone who says that he or she feels stressed by volunteering. Rather, people look forward to it. And the more they do it, the more they love it.

Additionally, Sneed's research has shown that adults over 50 who volunteer at least 200 hours a year have a lower risk of high blood pressure.

"If you think about people who have gone through life transitions like retirement, becoming bereaved, or no longer having children in the home, they might not have social connections they once had," Sneed said. "Doing volunteer work is a way to replenish those social ties."

Let's not forget the age old wisdom either that "if you don't lose it, you lose it." Or maybe, "If you rest, you rust."

Volunteering keeps you active, so you are less likely to do either.

Nourishing the Soul

If all of that is not enough, then consider this: Volunteering and random acts of kindness of most any kind stimulate the same pleasure centers of the brain associated with food and sex. In other words, helping others provides a natural high.

Chapter 11
Empathy and Smiles

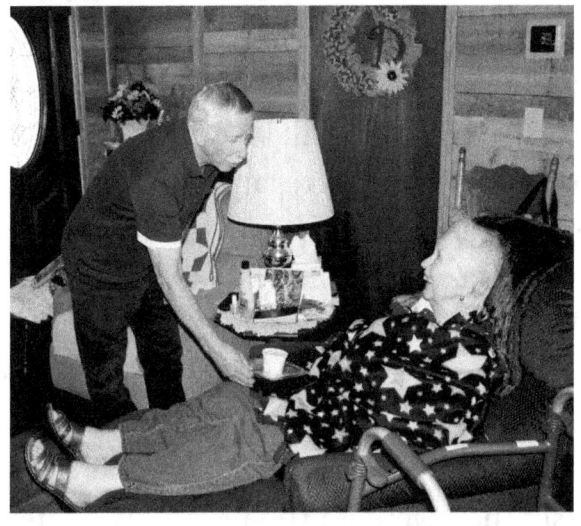

Volunteers and meal recipients become friends.

Charlie Boyer's grandson was standing beside him when a man in his underwear opened the door to receive his meal.

"I wish that I hadn't seen that," the 12-year-old said later. "Why would he do that?"

As someone who's delivered meals for more than eight years, I've had similar encounters and wondered the same thing. One involved leopard print undies. But with experience comes tolerance, understanding-—and a sense of humor.

That young man will be well ahead of most of his peers in that regard because of what his grandparents have—if you will excuse the pun—"exposed" him to.

"We thought delivering meals would be a good thing for the grandchildren to experience, and it has been," Charlie said.

Wife Jeanne added, "Results were mixed at first. They were a little fearful. But after we got them to go to the doorways with us and they saw how appreciative people are and after people started making over them, they were hooked."

As Charlie explained about delivering meals, "you definitely develop a greater empathy for people who can't get out and do things."

Part II: For What It's Worth

That includes the realization that just getting to the door can be an ordeal for some. "I noticed that Jeanne tells them, 'Take your time,' and I started doing that too," he said.

Empathy extends to picking up newspapers for them and gathering the mail, especially if it's in a box some distance from the door. Charlie's also concerned about safety, especially for those who live alone.

"If I see that someone is there who's not usually there, I'll ask them (meal recipients) who is visiting, just to be certain that no one is intruding on them," he said.

He's also stopped at a small, weathered house not on their assigned route to give an extra meal to an elderly woman who was sitting on the porch.

As they've delivered 40-plus meals every other week for more than four years, Charlie added that he's noticed "there are a certain number of people who are very lonely.

"Some are okay with that," he said. "But some are lost. There are enough places and ways for people to be involved that it shouldn't be that way. But it is.

"I feel that we're doing something good for 90 percent of the people we see," he continued. "But I'm confused about the other 1 out of 10. I don't know what their deeper need is. They just don't have the spirit and it's sad to see people like that.

"But the majority do have spirit and that makes you feel good about what you're doing. I always greet everyone with expectations that I can get them to smile and usually I can."

Chapter 12
Four-Legged Friends

Volunteers often bring treats to dogs like Izzy when they deliver meals.

When I first started delivering Meals on Wheels, I quickly discovered another reason to like dogs. They're loyal, loving, and constant companions for many who are homebound and otherwise live alone.

As soon as I realized that so many of those on my route had dogs, I started delivering canine treats as well as meals. Quickly, one of my favorites became Izzy, a little white-haired mop of a dog that came charging out the door to get her biscuit as soon as her owner opened it to receive his meal. She danced around my feet and made us both laugh, as I petted her and finally gave her the goody.

Unfortunately, her owner's health began to decline, and often a home care worker came to the door to receive the meal. Much of the time, Izzy wasn't with her. And when I asked why, she told me that the little dog was in bed with her owner. In other words, she was sacrificing her opportunity for a treat to be where she was needed. I started giving treats for Izzy to the worker, along with the meals.

Because of the treats and possibly because they sensed my fondness for them, nearly all of the dogs on my route quickly warmed up to me, even a Chihuahua named "Baby." Chihuahuas

Part II: For What It's Worth

are more often yappy, aggressive, and irritating than friendly. But Baby was the exception.

One day, though, Baby wasn't there. She and her owner usually were waiting for me outside, where he could smoke. Her owner was a big guy with a ponytail and I suspected that he probably rode a motorcycle during his younger years.

Before I could ask about the dog, he said, "Baby's dead. I fell on her and killed her."

How do you respond to news like that? I was so shocked and so saddened for him—both for his loss and for how it happened—that I must have said something in an attempt to console him. But I don't remember what.

He had gotten up during the night, he explained, tripped over the hose on his oxygen tank, and fell on her.

Two weeks later, I learned from a neighbor, Baby's owner had died. Was there a connection? I have no way of knowing. Aside from his need for the oxygen, he had seemed to be in reasonably good health. On the other hand, he continued to smoke. Possibly he died of respiratory failure. Or maybe it was something else. After all, we love our dogs as much as they love us.

That's certainly true for one of my meal recipients who is confined to a bed in her living room, where her friendly little dog remains her constant companion, with the affection of each for the other clearly visible. After I knock on door and enter, her buddy dances around on the bed, bolts to the floor to get a treat, and then returns to the bed. The brief moment of frantic excitement makes both of us smile and sometimes even laugh.

And I know that's the case for me and my dog, Pippa, an adult dog that I rescued six years ago. But I must admit that I also love another, White Cloud, who belongs to Betsy Wolf, a more recent addition to my Meals on Wheels route.

White Cloud is a 35-pound American Eskimo breed that sadly doesn't get enough exercise because of Betsy's limited mobility. He's well cared for, with plenty of shade and a wading pool to cool off in during hot weather, but he loves to run and play and the chain that he's on limits that considerably. Consequently, he's a frenetic bundle of energy, especially when he sees me arrive.

So I do more than just deliver a meal and a biscuit to Betsy and White Cloud. I spent some time with my four-legged buddy, giving him the affection and attention that he craves. And when cooler weather allows Pippa to travel with me, I let her out of the car to play with White Cloud as well.

Because of my special bond with White Cloud, one day Betsy asked me to help with her something. White Cloud has long, white hair and some of it had grown so long that it was, well, making for a messy situation when he performed a certain bodily function. She asked me to hold him while she cut his butt hair.

The good news is that none of us were injured.

When I returned to the center that day, I told Director Cher Robinson that I was going to have to ask for a raise.

Seriously, though, my life is richer not only because of the friends that I've made as I deliver meals to them, but because of their four-legged companions as well. Their dogs become my friends too and remind me of how much joy "man's best friend" brings to all of us, but especially for those who live alone, can't get out much, and become more isolated as they age.

An Indoor Swimming Pool?

Jeanne Boyer worried when one of her meal recipients didn't come to the door as quickly as he usually did.

"He was a gentleman who lived alone except for his dog," she remembered. "And he was one of my favorite guys."

Finally, he opened the door and quickly offered an apology. "I'm sorry he said. "I was feeding my turtles."

He then asked Jeanne if she'd like to see them, and she stepped inside his apartment.

"Right there in the middle of his living room was a child's-size swimming pool filled with dirt," she said. "It had rocks and plants. It was quite a setup."

And inside it, three box turtles were having lunch.

"One of them was named Larry," Jeanne recalled. "But I don't remember the names of the other two."

Larry was having a bad day, according to her friend.

"He had taken out a tunnel because he thought that it might be bothering the turtles," Jeanne explained. "But now Larry was going around and around, looking for it, and so he said that he was going to have to put the tunnel back in for him."

The man with the turtles no longer is on the Meals on Wheels route for Jeanne and Charlie Boyer, who deliver out of the Park Hills center, and she misses seeing him, Larry, and the other turtles.

"We love doing this and the people who receive the meals are just so appreciative," she said. "And it really disturbs us when someone goes off our route and we don't know why."

Chapter 13

Why We Volunteer

It's not for the money, nor for the fame.
It's not for any personal gain.
It's just for the love of fellow man.
It's just to lend a helping hand.
It's just to give a tithe of self.
That's something you can't buy
  with wealth.
It's not for the medals won with pride.
It's just for the feeling deep inside.
It's that reward deep in your heart.
It's the feeling you have been a part
of helping others far and near
that makes you be a volunteer.
—Anonymous

Someone asked me awhile back how long I had been volunteering. I'm almost never at a loss for words—ask my friends. But I was stunned to silence by that question. I had never thought about it. In asking others the same question, I've since learned that their reaction is much the same.

Volunteering is just something we do. Once you start doing it, it's as natural as eating, sleeping, and breathing. It becomes a part of you. As you do for others, you quickly recognize two things: How blessed you are and how much more there is that you can do to help others. And you want to do it.

There's nothing like volunteering to "develop an attitude of gratitude," according to my friend Caz Kenny, a recovering alcoholic who realized that "by helping others get sober, I was benefiting much more on an emotional and spiritual level…"

Lots of folks have developed that attitude by delivering meals and doing associated charitable work associated with the Bonne Terre, Park Hills, and other senior centers across the country. Just the few who helped me with this book found volunteering so rewarding that, collectively, they have been doing it for more than 100 years. Just imagine nationally what that total must be!

"Millions of volunteers enable 225 million meals to be delivered to 2.4 million seniors each year," according to Meals on Wheels America.

But that's just the meals aspect of the equation. Once you've discovered that "attitude of gratitude" by delivering food to others, you want to do more and, as you do so, you make the world a better place for everyone. Here's what others have to say about why they volunteer:

Mike and Jeainia Jennings

When they delivered meals to "Sweet Marie," Mike and Jeainia knocked on the door and then entered, as she requested. Often, she was in her favorite chair, with the television blasting, because she didn't hear well.

Well over 90, Marie lived alone and had only a niece, who visited weekly, as family.

"As soon as she saw us, she would jump up and grab my hand and lead me into the kitchen," Jeainia remembered. "She'd hold my hand as we talked and she'd tell me about her life, like where she went to school in rural Bonne Terre and how she worked for a utility company on the main street."

When time came for the couple to continue their Meals on Wheels route, Marie often grasped Jeainia's hand and asked that they stay a little longer.

"She probably didn't weigh 100 pounds, but her grip was intense," she said.

"We knew that it was company and human touch that she needed. She even asked for our phone number and would call me when she heard I was sick," she continued.

"She would embrace me as I left and tell me that she loved me. As the years passed, we loved her as much as she loved us."

In fact, they started ending their brief weekly visits with declarations of affection:

"Love you."

"Love you too."

In August 2016, Sweet Marie died.

But Mike and Jeainia still wave and call her name when they pass her house.

Part II: For What It's Worth

"That's why we do this," Jeainia explained. "Along with a meal, we want to deliver a touch of companionship, if only for a short while each day.

"We do this to see their smiles as they open their doors, to exchange 'hellos,' and to listen to a tale about how their week has gone."

In doing so, she added, they are receiving much more from the Meals on Wheels program than they are receiving.

"It is an honor and privilege to be part of this great program," she said. "Everyone needs that human contact, and it's a really great feeling to do this for them. It fills our hearts with appreciation, gratitude, compassion, and, sometimes, even love."

Al and Rena Ziegler

The retired teachers started delivering meals in 2003. Right now, they're volunteering twice a week, and, for awhile, they did it for three.

"I love it. If I had the time, I'd do it more," Rena said. "It's just really enjoyable doing something for someone else. I think that I get more out of it than the people who get the meals."

Al echoed Rena's words, adding, "It's a way to get out and see people and stay active. I love it."

Like many other volunteers, Al also revealed that he's occasionally assisted meal recipients with other things as well, including moving furniture and taking a mattress to the Goodwill store.

"A lot of people (who receive meals) don't see anyone else all day long," Rena said, adding that often friendships develop with these people who might otherwise feel alone and forgotten.

"Of course, you have your favorites," she said with a smile.

Joan Tebbenhoff

Volunteer Joan Tebbenhoff has made it her mission to introduce more people to what senior centers have to offer.

"My avocation is to help out wherever I can, and my main purpose here is to get people into the center," said Joan, who is 87 and has been volunteering at the Bonne Terre Senior and Nutrition Center since 1994. She also serves as secretary of the Ministerial Alliance and assists at the Helping Hands Ministries Thrift Store.

"We have a wonderful facility here, but people think that it's for the poor. It's not. It's for seniors," she added. "But it's like pulling teeth to get people to come in and see for themselves. A lot of people in Bonne Terre just won't do it."

Joan delivered meals occasionally in the past, but mostly she's worked at the front desk, providing information, counting money, and registering people. "I track 'em down when they don't sign in," she laughed.

Also, she's always looking for new ways to get more seniors in to socialize and enjoy the spacious center that adjoins city hall, and she solicits merchants for the prizes awarded during the bingo games that are some of the most popular activities.

"This helps me as I help others," Joan said. "It helps keep my mind active."

Part II: For What It's Worth

Charlie and Jeanne Boyer

"Jeanne drafted me, and I said that I'd give it a try," Charlie said, recalling when he and his wife started delivering meals out of the Park Hills center.

More than four years later, he judges the experience as "nothing but good.

"I didn't have any expectations," he said. "I just thought that it was something good to do because there's a need. But after doing it and seeing the smiles on people's faces, doing it makes me feel good and I really look forward to seeing those smiles."

Jeanne explained that she realized that delivering meals was something that she wanted to do as she worked as a nurse. "We got a little taste of what hungry people go through in the emergency room," she said.

Today, delivering a meals is a top priority for both.

"Everyone knows that's what Chuck and Jeanne do on every other Wednesday," the retired nurse said. "We'll even rearrange vacations and schedules so we don't miss.

"All the people who are doing this are volunteers and we don't want to have to put them in the position of filling in for us.

"Holly (Buxton, Park Hills director) and all the other people at the center are just so loving and caring, and we love doing this," she said.

Who Are the Volunteers?

"We have people who have to scrape money together to deliver meals and we have doctors and lawyers. We have all kinds, and we love them all," said Holly Buxton, director of the Park Hills center.

You Are Appreciated!

To those above and everyone else who volunteers, Bonne Terre Director Cher Robinson offers this reminder:

"Each and every one of you is very dear to us, and especially to the people whom you deliver to. We received many calls about how much we are appreciated, but it's truly *you* who makes the difference.

Part II: For What It's Worth

"It's your kindness, dedication, smiles, and caring and giving hearts that make this possible. We cannot express enough how much we appreciate what you do. Together, we make a fantastic team!"

Part III
Center Stage

Chapter 14
What You're Missing

Bonne Terre center's annual Christmas party provides plenty of good times and laughter.

Seven of us had just finished a laughter-filled meal as Bob Belsey, who used to play professionally in Los Angeles, began a lunchtime serenade on the piano, including one of my favorites, "Unchained Melody."

"That's so wonderful," someone said, adding that the piano sat mostly unused for years until Bob became a recent regular.

About the same time, Bob LeGesse brought in a bouquet of roses sent over to the Bonne Terre center by Dotty at Country Mart grocery store.

"There's so much positive energy here today. I just love it!" exclaimed Cher Robinson, who, as director, contributes significantly to that upbeat atmosphere, as does Holly Buxton at the Park Hills center.

"She's just awesome. We love her," said Jeanne Boyer. "It's not unusual for Holly to deliver meals too, if she's needed. And if we have a concern on our route about someone, she knows who we are talking about."

Many of us who volunteer hang around the center for awhile after we deliver meals. We do so to have lunch with friends, often friends that we've made because of the center, and to partake of that positive energy.

But there's room for many more to join us at senior centers all over the country. Sadly, many don't because of misconceptions about what they are and who they serve.

"Lots of people believe that the centers are for poor people," Holly said. "That's not true."

At the Bonne Terre Center, volunteer Joan Tebbenhoff echoes that sentiment and has made it her mission to educate seniors who are missing out. "Some people just won't check it out," she said. "It's so frustrating."

Possibly the misconception exists because Meals on Wheels programs, which are focused on helping those in need, operate out of senior centers.

But in terms of the centers themselves, the key word is "senior." Centers are multi-purpose gathering places for seniors of all income brackets. Yes, they provide meals, but they also assist with health needs and questions and tax concerns. They offer educational programs and recreational opportunities. They play host to and/or sponsor fun-filled events as fundraisers, including Bonne Terre's annual quilt show and bake sale during the summer and Park Hills' wild and crazy "Cruisin' for a

Cause, which involves the entire community, during fall.

In its inaugural during 2018, the event made $10,000 for the center, Director Holly Buxton said, adding she had even greater expectations for 2019, with many more events planned. They included car and dog shows, barbeque competition, beer garden, craft booths, and even an I Love Lucy Look Alike Contest.

In explaining how funds raised are used, Holly pointed out that about 300 meals a day, five days a week, are prepared, both for Meals on Wheels deliveries and for those who visit the center. "People are shocked when I tell them that we spent $3,000 to $4,000 a week on food," she said.

But just as important as we age, these centers are key places to reconnect with old friends and/or to make new ones. In fact, Meals on Wheels America says that 8 out of 10 people who enjoy a meal at their senior centers see friends more often than they would if they did not.

Part III: Center Stage

Sisters (from left) Deanna Vallo and Mona Miller are regulars at the Bonne Terre center. Sometimes volunteer Jeainia Jennings stops by to provide shoulder massages.

Sisters Mona Miller and Deanna Vallo and Nile Meyer are three who would agree with that. They're as regular at the Bonne Terre center as Cliff and Norm were at the bar in the television series "Cheers."

Usually sometime before 10 a.m., they arrive, claim their table near a window, grab coffee or ice tea, and then sit down to talk and laugh, not only among the themselves, but with others who decide to join them or just stop by to say hello. Sometimes, shoulder massages are exchanged as well!

One of each week's highlights occurs on Wednesday, when Rick, a salesman, stops by the center. "He comes over and hugs us!" Deanna said with a sly grin, and Mona enthusiastically agreed.

"My husband used to come here all the time with his brother," Mona remembered. "And I got onto him because I thought it was just for poor people.

"But then he passed away and I got back with Deanna and we've been coming here since 2005 or 2006, nearly every day."

Both Deanna and Nile delivered meals when they were younger and more mobile. "I try to come in every day, but I've fallen a few times recently," said Nile, who emphasized that he intends to live to be 100 years old.

After Mona echoed that sentiment, sister Deanna added, "I just hope that I make it through Saturday night!" That's when she was headed up to St. Louis to see a Cardinals baseball game.

Part III: Center Stage

The sisters are big fans. "But I've never seen 'em win," Mona lamented. Fortunately, though, it isn't just about winning for the elder of the two sisters.

"After my husband died, I said that no other man could put his shoes under my bed unless they belonged to Jim Edmonds (former centerfielder for the Cardinals)," she said with a hearty laugh.

For Mona's 80th birthday, her daughter had a cake designed with a little bed on top and a pair of baseball cleats under it.

Chapter 15

Senior Center Facts

Bonne Terre's facility is one of about 10,000 senior centers across the country that prepare meals daily, both for visitors and Meals on Wheels recipients.

The National Council on Aging reports that more than one million older Americans are served daily by about 10,000 senior centers across the country.

Participants

- Approximately 70 percent of senior center participants are women; half of them live alone.
- The majority are Caucasian, followed by African Americans, Hispanics, and Asians respectively.
- Compared with their peers, senior center participants have higher levels of health, social interaction, and life satisfaction and lower levels of income.
- The average age of participants is 75.
- 75 percent of participants visit their center 1 to 3 times per week. They spend an average of 3.3 hours per visit.

Senior center services

- Senior centers serve as a gateway to the nation's aging network, connecting older adults to vital community services that can help them stay healthy and independent.
- More than 60 percent of senior centers are designated focal points for delivery

of Older Americans Act services, allowing older adults to access multiple benefits in one place.
- Senior centers offer a wide variety of programs and services, including:
  - Meal and nutrition programs
  - Information and assistance
  - Health, fitness, and wellness programs
  - Transportation services
  - Public benefits counseling
  - Employment assistance
  - Volunteer and civic engagement opportunities
  - Social and recreational activities
  - Educational and arts programs
  - Intergenerational programs

How are senior centers funded?

To maintain operations, senior centers must leverage resources from a variety of sources. These include federal, state, and local governments; special events, public and private grants, businesses, bequests, participant contributions, in-kind donations, and volunteer hours. Most centers rely on 3 to 8 different funding sources.

Benefits and impact

- Research shows that older adults who participate in senior center programs can learn to manage and delay the onset of chronic disease and experience measurable improvements in their physical, social, spiritual, emotional, mental, and economic well-being.
- Today's senior centers are reinventing themselves to meet the needs and desires of the aging baby boom generation. Boomers now constitute more than two-thirds of the 50+ popula-

tion. Senior centers are developing new programs and opportunities for this dynamic generation of older adults.

Chapter 16

The Quiet Man

Bob LaGesse with his family of volunteers, (from left) Ava, Audrea, Alivia, and Stephanie.

Bob LaGesse doesn't have a loud voice or an eye-popping personality.

But the slender man with glasses and a baseball cap "is a super person who does so much for us and is so quiet about it," according to Cher Robinson, director of the Bonne Terre center.

"I love to do things for the seniors," said the man who is himself 77 and estimated that he has been helping out in one way or another "almost every day" for 15 years.

"I enjoy seeing this place (center) grow," he said. "And, when someone asks, I don't know how to say no."

Often, no one needs to ask. If Bob sees a need or opportunity, he acts. One of his latest missions is to get handicap buttons installed on the two sets of heavy double doors at the entrance to the center.

For seven years, he's made a 286-mile round trip four or five times a season to Campbell, MO, to buy fresh produce and bring it back to the center, at his own expense. As a result of his generosity, seniors and others can buy at a reduced cost some of the best-tasting watermelons, cantaloupes, and peaches in the nation, with all proceeds going to the center, which operates primarily on donations and contributions.

Bob also has built seven huge room dividers so the center can play host to several events at once and racks to hang the dozens of quilts brought in for the annual quilt show and bake sale fundraiser.

"If the good Lord gives you something that you're good at, you just do it," said the man who has rheumatoid arthritis but "keeps moving all the time" instead of taking medications as a means of coping with it.

He also "fixes things in the kitchen," and delivers meals every Wednesday, while filling in on other days.

"It only takes about an hour to deliver meals," he said.

But on a recent Tuesday, when he was asked to fill in on a route that he hadn't traveled in awhile, he was gone for more than two hours. That was because he and the people on that route "had to catch up," he explained with a smile.

Additionally, Bob has made helping out at the center a family affair, and emphasized that encouraging children to do charitable work "is what it's all about." For example, grandson Brody sometimes accompanies him to Campbell and helps load and unload the melons, following in the footsteps of older Brady, who did so as well.

Meanwhile, granddaughter Ava helps deliver meals when she's not in school and, along with her sister, Alivia, cleans up in the dining area following monthly evening meals or on special occasions.

"A lot of people praise them and give them a dollar and they didn't expect anything like that," Bob said. "That helps them see that they're really doing something."

Daughter Audrea and daughter-in-law Stephanie help out with fundraisers, such as the bake sale, and occasionally assist in the kitchen.

"We couldn't have done the (benefit) cookbook without Stephanie," said volunteer and friend Shirley Christopher.

By the way, Bob credits Shirley with getting him into the center as a regular. "I enjoyed it," he remembered. "So I started bringing my Dad, and he liked it. Every day, then, he started reminding me that it's 'time to eat.'"

Part III: Center Stage

Bob laughed at the memory, and suggested that possibly the food wasn't his father's only reason. "Dad liked the ladies," he said.

Chapter 17
Aging Matters

"Mr. Moss would rather sing hymns than eat! We loved his singing and Joann's playing! What sweet people we have at the center. Truly blessed to know so many wonderful seniors!"
–Holly Buxton, director Park Hills Senior and Nutrition Center.

Bonne Terre, Park Hills and other area senior centers are affiliated with Aging Matters.

Also known as Southeast Missouri Area Agency on Aging, it is a not-for-profit organization serving an 18-county area in Southeast Missouri, with the regional office in Cape Girardeau.

"The essential goal of our organization is to provide quality services to enhance the health, safety, and well-being of persons, age 60 and over, enabling them to live in their own homes for as long and independently, as possible," the organization said.

"Because our major financial support is through the Older Americans Act, donations are an important funding source," it added. "Your help through donations, gift giving, and business sponsorships enables us to continue providing the much needed services to the seniors in our region."

An 18-member board of directors governs the agency. One delegate from each county is elected by area adults, 60 years of age and older.

You can contact Aging Matters by e-mail at info@agingmatters2u.com or phone at (573) 335-3331 or (800) 392-8771.

Chapter 18

Who Is Eligible for Meals?

Cleanup crew Ava, Alivia, and Natelie following monthly evening meal at Bonne Terre center.

Meals on Wheels recipients must be considered "home-bound" and 60 years of age or older or 18 to 59, disabled, and living in senior housing, either with a qualifying senior or in apartments exclusively for seniors.

The program is *not* income based.

At centers, meanwhile, qualified participants must be 60 years of age or older or 18 to 59 and disabled. Those who don't qualify still can dine at centers as guests, and they are charged for their meals.

Donations are appreciated from both those who receive meals at home and those who dine in the centers. But no qualifying person is charged for meals. Most of those who are homebound are financially unable to contribute.

Chapter 19

Bonne Terre Center History

Volunteers Neil Gunn and Renee Mullen leave the Bonne Terre center to deliver meals.

Originally, the Bonne Terre center functioned as a satellite of the Park Hills center. Volunteers from Bonne Terre picked up meals there to deliver to home-bound residents of their community.

In 1985, the Bonne Terre center opened at 420 N. Long St., near the city park and just across the street from long-time volunteer Dorothy Gouin, who was the inspiration for this book. With kitchen equipment available, cooked food then was brought over from Park Hills, where it was packaged for Meals on Wheels and placed in hot and cold holding tables for those who dined at the center.

In 1988, the center became independent, with meals prepared on site.

The center was relocated to its current location at 114 N. Allen St. in 2016, thanks to the generosity of Sharo Shirshekan, who had bought and renovated old Bonne Terre Junior High School and donated the buildings to the city. The fire department, police department, and city hall now are located there, as well as the spacious center and senior apartments.

For too many seniors in and around Bonne Terre, the center still is an undiscovered treasure.

About the Author

Nourishing the Soul is the 12th book for author Robert U. Montgomery, who has been a Meals on Wheels volunteer since early 2011.

Two illustrated children's books are his latest commercial offerings. With **Who Let the Bugs Out?** and **Who Let the Frogs Out?**, he hopes to encourage children to spent more time outside playing and learning about nature. They are mysteries flavored with humor and include important life lessons as the mysteries are solved.

Montgomery also is the author of books about fishing, nature, dogs, and nostalgia, as well as two eco-thriller novels involving wolves. His books are available from Amazon, as well as from other retailers.

His **RUM Publishing** website features blogs about nature, as well as more detailed information about his books. Additionally, he is an award-winning freelance writer and photographer and a Senior Writer for B.A.S.S. Publications.

Montgomery lives in the rural community of Terre du Lac, Mo., with his rescue dog Pippa, who co-authored the book *Pippa's Journey*. She also accompanies him on his Meals on Wheels deliveries.

www.ingramcontent.com/pod-product-compliance
Lightning Source LLC
Chambersburg PA
CBHW052057070526
44584CB00017B/2217